Lazarus Man
"Return to the Howard Universe"

Nelson Jackson

PublishAmerica
Baltimore

© 2010 by Nelson Jackson.
All rights reserved. No part of this book may be reproduced, stored in a retrieval system or transmitted in any form or by any means without the prior written permission of the publishers, except by a reviewer who may quote brief passages in a review to be printed in a newspaper, magazine or journal.

First printing

PublishAmerica has allowed this work to remain exactly as the author intended, verbatim, without editorial input.

Hardcover 978-1-4512-8238-2
Softcover 978-1-4512-8237-5
PUBLISHED BY PUBLISHAMERICA, LLLP
www.publishamerica.com
Baltimore

Printed in the United States of America

References:

*Written permission for the use of names has been obtained for all persons in the book unless they are deceased or purposely omitted.

Acknowledgements

Generally most authors start their acknowledgements by giving honor to all of the people who have contributed to their book. In no small measure do I deny that everything contained herein came about as a life long collaborative effort to my self- actualization. I have gleaned ideas and outlooks from many experiences over the course of a lifetime. To all the people who have been in my life, I thank you. Years ago I said if I ever have the means to throw a party like a living wake, I will put an advertisement in the newspaper inviting all of my friends; if you have doubts about our friendship, don't come. Those of you who truly believe you know me will have no problem identifying yourself as my friend. It may be a small party.

My wife Carol, my daughter Natalie and my son Nelson Jr. are really the only people who have a clue about my motives, my beliefs and my unsung accomplishments. It is to and for them that I dedicate not only this book, but everything that in my human capacity to give is for them. To my brother Edward thanks for being a big brother through the good times and bad times. Thank you all for being the most important thing in my life.

To the students of Howard University; the title *Lazarus Man*, can not truly convey what you give me everyday we are together. There is no place I would rather be and there are no people I would rather be with; our bond will transcend generations. Special thanks to all of the professors and support people who have made this experience seamless. You have inspired me to do things and conceptualize ideas I had long thought dead.

Contents

Chapter 1 13

Chapter 2 26

Chapter 3 36

Chapter 4 41

Chapter 5 46

Chapter 6 52

Chapter 7 57

Chapter 8 63

Chapter 9 68

Chapter 10 72

Lazarus Man
"Return to the Howard Universe"

Nelson Jackson

Chapter 1

Returning back to school to attend college on a campus as a student after a 35 years absence literally scared the hell out of me. Some of my sleepless thoughts included whether or not I would be welcome by the eleven thousand plus 18 to 25 year old young people who were competing with each other to graduate. Would I be called names like; the old man, gramps or worse the over-the-hill has-been?

Should I dress like my peers or should I dress age appropriately? Even though I didn't want to be ostentatious, I realized that either way I just wasn't going to just blend in. *Would wearing a suit and tie be condescending?* Since my days had to compartmentalized into being a full time student and trying to build a business, I finally reconciled that on the days when I had to leave school and attend meetings or go to places where professional attire is required, I would wear a suit, on other days I would dress fashionably casual mainly because that's what I had in my wardrobe. I certainly wasn't going to go out and buy 'school clothes'.

When I'm in class I have to remind myself to avoid being or sounding like an old sage. Easy on the anecdotes and stay away from phrases like "back in the day;" "the way we used to do it," and the worst of all; "it has been my experience"! I pride myself on being a pretty good listener, but now I need to be ten times better. I am not the professor and not there to teach. I am the student, my job is to learn. I can learn as much from the other students as I can from the professor by just listening and observing.

What if some young upstart challenges me in some rude or physical way? These are things I never tolerated in life, so now do I have to acquiesce to incivility to assimilate? The answer to that one came easy, because I know that I cannot change. Let the chips fall where they may. Each situation, if it happens, will have to be dealt with by the appropriate response. End of story! This 57 year old man is only going to take so much hazing, which is none.

Can I handle the task of studying for long hours and be able to work my schedule into the demands of being a fledgling business owner, a husband, a father, a community activist and still have enough life left for a little me time? My wife thinks I'm a busy body and she tells me I'm happiest when I piddling with something. Now I won't run out of things to piddle with, after all I'm the guy who agrees with Paris Hilton, "Being bored is a sin." I have no excuses for not having anything to do. The secret will be time management.

What does my wife and kids really think about my decision to go back to school? The economy is in the tank, our personal wealth and income is on life support and I ain't getting any younger. My son who is an Iraq/Afghanistan veteran has his own plate full because he's trying to go to college and decide what to do with his life. He doesn't really know what his Dad's latest Don Quixotic experiment is right now. My daughter who is a grad student at the Corcoran School of Art and Design, a Nuevo hippie and a daddy's girl, thinks it's the greatest thing in the world. My wife can be very stoic so hers is the read I need to decipher most. A lot of responsibility is on her shoulders and she will be the person to cover my lapses in time, tasks and sometimes money. Can and will she do it? My wife is a unique spouse because never in our twenty seven years of marriage has she stifled me from doing what I wanted to do. She has always been supportive, but she demands practicality, which makes her an excellent partner. She's not afraid to tell me when I'm in over the top. Basically I have a green light from the home front, but I know I'm under a microscope. One of my goals is not to run the bus into a bridge.

My personal health issues! As a cancer survivor and a person with a stent in the main artery coming from my heart, am I up to the additional stress physically? That one came easy for me to answer as well. Just like my father, I want to go out with my boots on, not sitting in a chair watching the grass grow. Just ain't gonna happen! Besides I have hundreds of things I want to do and they won't get done by wishing and hoping. I wrote a poem back when I was in my late teens called 'The First Step'.

The first step in a journey
Is sometimes hard to take
But the more you want to get somewhere
The easier it is to make

So when you think that you must go
To places new and strange
Pick up one foot and then the other
And quickly things will change.

This has always been my mantra.

As much as I like to think that I don't give a damn about what other people think, deep down inside we all care, just some less then others. What will my friends and extended family think? Here's the list, it will be brief!

Mother-in-law: "I always thought he was a crazy fool. He needs to get a job with the Post Office. What exactly does he do anyway?"

My mother (Beginning stages of dementia): "That's nice! What are you doing again? Don't get in with the wrong crowd at school."

My oldest brother: "That's great; let me know if you need my help?"

A potential business partner and good friend, Robert Greene; "Fantastic, I'm really happy for you".

A potential business partner and good friend, Marleen Aldana: "How do you translate that into making money? Que tal amigo?"

My cousin-in-law: "Jack! There are some fine mommas on that campus. I never know what to expect from you".

The rest I never give much stock to in the first place. If I'm successful then they'll be on the front line and if I fail they will be front liners.

A lot of other thoughts went through my head that night. After keeping my wife awake till after midnight, I got up to inventory my back pack for the fifth or sixth time in the previous two weeks. Pencils, pens, portfolio, tooth brush, lotion, spot remover, change of underwear, extra necktie, shirt, finger nail file, Leatherman, and a small flashlight (I don't know why). My acceptance letter in case anyone challenged me.

I promised my wife I would take the Metro instead of driving, because there is no place to park and she draws the line on parking tickets. I got ready at 5AM, showered, changed clothes twice, fixed a lunch to take and went to the bus stop. Not only was this my first day back to school, but I had not ridden a Metro bus in a few years. First surprise! The bus was as quiet as a morgue and everyone except me seemed to be quite used to each other. To the driver I was just another fare. I was an outsider, but as time went on I was grafted into the group. I caught the subway at the Silver Spring Metro Station and was probably mistaken for all of the regular commuters. Little did they know I was off on one of the great adventures of my life. Since I left home two hours before my first class, I had some time to kill. My daughter was a legendary Starbucks patron when she went to school at Howard, so I thought I would follow her lead, in spite of the fact I hate trendy places. My soldier instincts kicked in and I began to make mental notes of everything and everyone around me. I seemed to blend in as just another face in the crowd which helped defuse some of my anxiety. I looked over my schedule for the 100th time and started to make my way to campus, a half hour early for my first class. A soldier should always be at least 15 minutes early and that discipline paid off. My first class was not meeting where it was supposed to be and there was no one around to tell me where they would be meeting. I guess I missed the memo. Mildly in a panic, I quickly regrouped and remembered that the Political Science office was on the ground floor. Lucky for me a lady was in the office early, because they were not due to open for another hour. She put me at ease and looked up the class location by the name of the professor. She told me where the class would be held and told me to tell the professor that he was "on her list" for not telling her that he had moved the class location. I didn't do it. I wasn't going to start my first day by carrying a threat to the professor. So far this wasn't so bad. I had solved my first problem and passed my first test which was getting to the right class on time.

What was my class going to be like? It was a political science class so this should be an easy "A" for me. After all I come from a political background and I've been political all my life. Will the other students recognize my superior political intellect? Will they hang on my every word? Aren't they lucky to have me! Would my professor just throw up his hands and say "Nelson, you don't have to come to class if you don't want to, I know you already know all this stuff? Wrong, wrong and more wrong!

I took my seat in the first row, first seat by the door. I wanted to have an easy escape route if something went wrong and I was embarrassed beyond composure. As the other students began filing in, some very late, I had a chance to eyeball all of them and make my mental notes. Tall and slim, nice hair, fancy dresser, a little arrogant, loud and obnoxious, cute and pixy-like, mature and worldly, these are just some of my first impressions, which would later come unraveled like a ball of string. For example cute and pixy would turn out to be short and snotty, loud and obnoxious turned out to be considerate and helpful and fancy dresser it was rumored had a night job if you get my meaning. I had been mistaken for the professor by a few of my classmates and that turned out to be more of a burden than an asset. Some students thought I had inside influence with the professors or that I could read their minds, which was not even close to being true.

In walks my first professor, a Nigerian PhD. who had the regal arrogance of most successful Nigerians and a strong gait of confidence. Since I had traveled while in the Army and had done a lot of work with immigrants in my professional life, I had my own private stereotypes. Wrong assumptions again! Dr. Ifedi introduced himself and gave a brief synopsis of what was expected and what he wanted to be accomplished. He made it perfectly clear what it would take to get an "A" and what was the easiest way to fail. He interspersed his lecture with a satirical sense of humor that if you weren't paying attention would go right over your head. That was right up my alley, because educated humor is the best kind and separates the thinkers from the sleepers. Within the first fifteen minutes I realized I was going to like him. I have a habit of paying close attention to speakers since I have had to speak publicly on many occasions. I trained myself when I was in the Army that paying attention to detail may save my life. Dr. Ifedi would turn out to be interesting and knowledgeable and required my undivided attention. In his class nothing could be taken for granted.

The first task for the class was for everyone to introduce themselves and he started at the opposite end of the room, which meant that I would be last. Most of the states in the country were represented by the students, including several foreign countries. There were some interesting and colorful background stories. When my turn finally came, I gave my name, mentioned my family, stated that I was a former student returning and said that I had my own business. Dr. Ifedi concluded by saying something to the effect that I might be the person to know for those who wanted to be rich business people or needed a job. That got a chuckle out of all of us and from that first day we had formed ourselves into a class with common bonds, despite age, gender or any of those other things that seem to separate people.

Nine o'clock came and I had ten minutes to get to my next class. Spanish I; a brand new frontier and I found myself praying "God has not given me the spirit of fear, but power, love and a sound mind..." In other words, help me Jesus! I had taken Latin and French in high school, 30 plus years ago and was identified in an Army diagnostic test as having a propensity to learn languages fairly easily. All that being said, at 57, I wasn't that confident that my brain was elastic enough to catch on as quickly as a 19 year old. This class I knew would be my kryptonite and I would have to devote a large percentage of my study time to get at least a "C". I was delightfully pleased that my professor was beautiful Panamanian woman who had all of the attributes I find attractive in Latin women. She was feisty, matter of fact, no-nonsense and theatrical. No problem paying attention in this class, now all I had to do is not make a complete fool of myself.

I had forgotten one very important fact about language classes. The serious teachers almost always talk in the subject language for everything. I didn't know any useful Spanish and I had to rely on all of my wits to make out what she was instructing. Almost all of the other students in the class had taken Spanish in high school and they had a foundation to build upon. I began to curse myself silently because I had previously managed an office of bilingual employees for 7 years and I didn't have the sense to teach myself the language. My egalitarian attitude in the office was to let their cultural bonds go without intrusion by a boss whose goal might be to convict them by their words. That worked pretty well as a manager, but was not worth a dime now.

Professora Bolton turned out to be patient with me and I made sure she recognized that I was taking this class out of necessity, not just because I needed to fulfill a language requirement to graduate. I have a strong attachment to the Latin community and I am a strong supporter of Hispanic rights. My future aspirations are intrinsically tied to that community and I am glad to be a part of the bridge that seeks to bring the African-American and Hispanic communities together. Together we will be a force to be reckoned with. (Forgive my pontification; this is an issue I'm very passionate about.)

Spanish class was everything I expected as far as the amount of effort I would need to pass the class successfully and then some. In order to keep up, I bought supplemental Spanish books, attended a lecture for extra credit and visited the professor in her office on two occasions to make sure I was on track. Ultimately the extra effort paid off.

That was my first day in those two classes which began on a Monday, which left me 5 business hours left in the day. My Tuesday schedule was equally exciting as it was challenging. My schedule consisted of a 10AM political science class, an 11:30 class of poetry writing and a 12:30 class of Humanities.

If this book is to benefit anyone who is seeking to return to school, there are other details that need to be acknowledged. Once I got accepted back into school my reaction was "oh s_ _t!" This is really happening. It all started very serendipitously. The company I had previously managed was having financial trouble and a lot of the blame lay with the owners who did not believe in self improvement and as a consequence put very little stock in education. The business suffered as a result. I saw the recession coming long before it hit the news. When you're paycheck starts bouncing you don't need a house to fall on you. I became so unhappy with my employment life that I had begun to sink into depression and self destructive behavior. Not enough sleep, not eating properly, bad attitude and health issues. Basically I had reached the point where I said enough is enough. Using the little money I was receiving from unemployment, I began to get licensed in every area that I was eligible and as a result everyday I got a little stronger and more motivated to get into business for myself. I sat myself down and did some minor calculations just to figure out how much money I had made for other businesses that I did not own over the years. I had worked for companies that take as much government money as they can while at the same time complaining about government being too big. Bitterness aside, little did I know that some of the greatest opportunities I could not even predict would ever happen began to unfold. During this period of business building, I was able to go to the presidential inauguration of President Obama, which has deep rooted meaning to me and my family. My ancestors wanted me there. I was able to visit Dr. Dorothy Height in Howard Hospital a few days after her 98th birthday and a week before she died. I was able to attend her funeral at the National Cathedral. I was able to participate in economic development courses, attend business seminars and go to school with some of the most outstanding young people I will ever meet. Talk about turning lemons into lemonade!

Throughout the book I will bob and weave, back and forth on how returning to school was and continues to have the biggest impact on any success I have achieved in starting a business. I will prove that not only can it be done successfully; it is indispensable to understanding today's markets, the technology used and the demographics that will be vital to growing a business. One of my pet peeves has always been to avoid at all costs letting age cloud the joy of thinking young. Old people with old thinking are not welcome in my world. Innovation requires fresh thinking and fresh thinking begins with youth or at the very least older people who can appreciate youthfulness.

First class on Tuesday and Thursdays with Dr. Alicia Petersen was an instant connection because she has an easy going, empathetic attitude that does not reveal any judgmental prejudices. I rightly predicted that some of my younger classmates might mistake her kindness for weakness and that turned out to be a losing proposition for some at grade time. Dr. Petersen has strong beliefs about the values of community development. I'm not sure if she has done it by herself, but now Howard University has made community development a minor discipline. In her own right, Dr. Petersen has strong connections to Capital Hill, which is invaluable to teaching students the nuances of Washington politics. I felt I would do well in her class, but my motivation was not one of arrogance; rather that I can actually learn something. Hearing the viewpoint and experiences of a real Washington insider is vital in today's politics despite those that try to run as an outsider. Also I love anybody who walks the walk. I found out that somehow in her schedule she finds times to mentor young people from disadvantaged backgrounds. Basically she has 3 or 4 jobs going simultaneously, so if she can do it, why can't I. That's the kind of inspiration you can't get from a textbook.

My next class was a real hoot! It was entitled Creative Writing/ Poetry; featuring Dr. Tony Medina, truly one of a kind and an individual who is serious about the elevation of creative writing as an art form. He's one of those professors that every student needs to have at least once. Dr. Medina is a classic iconoclastic person; he will destroy your perceptions of yourself. I have been writing poetry since elementary school so I just knew this would be like dropping a fish in water. 'Not so fast Emerson!' The first thing he did was make us put our desks in a circle. Oh, oh, I thought, here goes Romper Room. I snapped back to reality when I recognized that this was a concept that my fellow dorm mates used to philosophize about back in the 70's. We came up with the idea during a night of heavy smoke inhalation, that Europeans i.e. "white people" (In the 70's everything was black vs. white.) liked to make buildings square, where you have corners and someone can be excluded or ignored in the group. In a circle everyone has to confront each other, visually, audibly and spiritually and there are no hiding places. Okay, maybe it was a slight flashback, but I understood the concept. During the class introductions, he had a comment to make about everyone, usually something that would knock you off your self-righteousness. When my turn came and after I concluded my brief bio, he said that probably, because I had worn a suit that day that he thought I might be a government agent sent to spy on the class. He said this jokingly. Once again he was another no nonsense professor and those that thought this was going to be a cakewalk would be brutally surprised. This guy takes his subject seriously. I guess that's why he has several books published to his credit. Even though I was older than him we have developed a bond of sorts and even though he is older that most of his students, he seems to be able to bridge both worlds seamlessly.

One of the cautions that I will give to my older fellow returning students is don't try to over justify why you are returning to school. I wasted breath in some classes by explaining that my company bids on government contracts and I was in between contracts. Nobody cares! One class I said that I had a made a promise to my parents that someday I would go back and finish; another big whop-tee-do. I mentioned that my daughter had graduated from Howard cum laude a year earlier and my son was in the 82nd Airborne, so what! I said in my bio in one class that I had been married for 27 years, but I didn't see any of the young coeds go; oh that's so sweet! Basically what I'm trying to say is that everyone in the class has a compelling story and even though you may have traveled around the sun a few more times then they have doesn't make you any more or less important, smarter or interesting. Trust me you will be much better off listening to some one else's story than putting yourself out there. Occasionally some of the students will come and ask you to tell more about yourself after class. Then it's okay! Otherwise open your ears more and keep your mouth closed. Its like advice for me, I don't offer it unless I'm asked! Some people I charge good money for it.

My next class turned out to be my Achilles heel; Humanities II. Even though I like Humanities and had a great professor for Humanities I, this class turned out to be the one that no matter what I wrote on my assignments, my writing style or content never seemed to make the grade except once or twice. I went to discuss my progress or the lack thereof on two occasions. He said he was highly critical to make us better writers. I guess the medicine didn't take very well, which us why I ended up with the only "C" grade that semester on my transcript. I was always engaged in the subject matter and read all of the material, but somehow this professor and I could not reach each other. Things happen! For the record this was the only professor that made references to my age in class and made me feel a little uneasy. I have been used to challenging people or people challenging me all my life. I figured out that the more I pushed in this class, the deeper the hole I was sinking into to. Unfortunately for me or perhaps fortunately, I was no virgin to what I perceived as our incompatibility. I regret that some of the things that I had experienced in school as one of the first black children to integrate the school system in Harford County, Maryland resurfaced. A person knows like any other animal when it is being pushed in an effort to prove that you don't fit within the paradigm. The point for now is you won't always be received as doing some noble thing by returning to school. Initially I thought that some of the students might think; why is this guy taking up valuable space. I didn't foresee that it might come from a professor.

When Friday came at the end of my first week, I felt like I had climbed Mt. Kilimanjaro, physically, emotionally and mentally. I had not devoted more than a couple of hours to my business that week, but I was walking on cloud nine. I think my wife probably recognized a change in me. I possessed that teenage drive, which is essential to being a success in school and in business. Looking back on it, I had worked at school and business from 5 in the morning until 9 at night and I slept like a baby for the first time in years. My personal health improved as well. I have increased appetite and I am getting regular cardio-vascular exercise from walking. Anyone that knows Howard's campus knows that coming from anywhere below Bryant Street, you have to traverse the hill from hell to get to the main campus. Just doing that is an accomplishment in its self.

There is one aspect you need to consider when you decide to return to school. Few people will share your sense of well being and accomplishment. Some people will be envious and some will think you are wasting your time. There will be those who will think that you are suffering from some form of mental illness, you will hear disparaging remarks being made behind your back. Ignore them! If your motive to return is because you're not out to prove anything to anyone but yourself, you will be a lot more comfortable with your decision. If you fail at your attempt then you will see a side of your family and friends that you wished would have remained hidden. Some will bask in your failure and some will use it as an excuse or a reason to not reach for a dream. You will be their personal icon of failure. This journey will be more personal than anything you may ever accomplish, but you can't project that feeling on anyone else. The end result will speak for itself. I like to think it's analogous to cooking. Your guests don't care how much work and preparation it took to get the food on the table; they have one thing in mind and that's to eat. The satisfaction comes from knowing what you put into the effort and the accolades don't just come from how the other person thinks it tastes, but how it tastes to you. Ultimately only you know what it took to get it to the table.

Chapter 2
What Happened 35 Years Ago...

When I left high school in the summer of 1971, my mind was racing at a thousand miles an hour. I had graduated from a one of the top private schools in the state of Maryland. I did it on my own terms, meaning I didn't always play by their rules or dance to the beat of their drum. During my junior and senior years I became self-radicalized by the fast changing pace of society. America was in the end stages of the Viet Nam War. The Civil Rights Movement was in full swing and the counter-culture revolution was psychedelic. I was in the middle of all three, but not always by choice.

Being an African-American male of draft age from a family with strong values about duty, honor and service was not easy. I remember well on the day of my 18th birthday my mother picked me up from school and drove me straight to the Draft Board office for registration. Like in the game Monopoly it was "do not stop or pass go and do not collect 200 dollars". In my family's mind, this is the right thing to do. I can't remember the exact date two or three weeks later, I received my draft classification of 1-A, which means in six weeks be ready to ship out. "And its one, two three, what are we fighting for? Don't ask me I don't give a damn, next stop is Viet Nam..." To add insult to injury this was a war I was deeply opposed to and had participated in many demonstrations against it.

My family and I were up to our heads in the Civil Rights Movement. My father served as President of the NAACP on at least two occasions. During his tenure he had several death threats and a cross was burned on our lawn. My mother was a closet feminist of sorts who believed in home and hearth, but she also believed in equality for women. I inherited their sense of no fear of confrontation. Since I had attended a high school of less than 5 Black male students by my graduation, I automatically was propelled to be a "Young Turk" in the struggle. It was my choice to go to private school and not my parents. There is an unwritten rule in our family then and now that when you make choices, you stick with them. My neighborhood friends and I talked a lot about the more radical methods of attaining equality by embracing the tenants of the Black Panther Party, the Student Non-Violent Coordinating Committee and the Weathermen. Most of it was just talk. Little did we know that integration was not the equation to equality? Later on we recognized that during this period it was more of, I want what they have from blacks and whites wanted to take a part in what we have. It is amazing how degradation and the blues can be so sexy. The civil rights struggle dominated a good part of your daily existence in those days and shaped the thinking of all of us, not always with positive results. Some of us paid a heavy price for our dedication and many still do.

Counter-culturism was another big cog in the wheel of socialization during the late 60's and early 70's. The slogan "Make love, not war" was in and I was all for it. Turn on, tune in and drop out was one of many miss-guided creeds during that time. A number of my peers chose to just drop out of society completely. Woodstock was the iconic event of the time and the Jimmy Hendrix experience was one of the icons of that shaped that period. Smoking marijuana went from not being cool, to being cool, to not being cool to whatever it is today; okay for medicinal purposes. I inhaled and I liked it back then.

Part of my integration experience was the secret dating of white girls. Interracial dating was taboo back then. I like to think that I did it to satisfy my natural curiosity. I wanted to know what the other side thinks, how the other side feels and what did the other side know that I didn't. It's true; it's all pink on the inside.

When I graduated in the summer of 71, I was a full blown hippie, civil rights radical and a person who questioned everything establishment. My first thought after high school was that college was a waste of time. I did not want to be transformed into a 9 to 5 automaton. I still feel that way and if I hear another black parent tell their child that you need to get a job with the post office again, I'm subject to go postal. There's a whole big world out there. Find something to do that makes you happy; because inevitably you're gonna die. I would jump off of the Calvert Street Bridge, if I wake up one morning and realized that I spent the better part of my life as a robot. Understand that it isn't easy swimming against the current of the status quo and you will get beaten up more times than you will win; but the victories are so sweet.

After floundering around on some small construction jobs during the summer of 71and blackening my lungs with THC, I woke up one morning in the fall when most of my fellow classmates had gone on to college, I said I need to go to school. Going on to college was a natural rite of passage for my family. My two older brothers were in college at the time; my father was a graduate of Virginia Union Theological Seminary in Richmond, Virginia and had met my mother there. Even though she did not graduate, she went on to graduate from Cortez Peters Business School and held professional positions throughout her working life. One of my aunts was one of the founders of one of the first "colored" schools in Harford County, Maryland. She was my mother's mentor.

I took my new found revelation about going to college for advice to my great-aunt on my father's side, Fanny Belle Moore Jackson, herself an educator for over 35 years. My Aunt Fanny was not a person to mince words and if you did not know her, you would think that every word out of her mouth was a scolding. That couldn't be farther from the truth. Prior to getting her blessing I knew I would get a stern tongue lashing. "What the hell were you thinking when you graduated from high school, that you had arrived?" (She didn't cuss, but you could feel the word hell in her tone.) Once the flames died down, she started formulating a plan; mind you all of this was going on while she was fixing me breakfast. "Your Dad is mad and disappointed in you. He had high hopes for you even though he would never tell you, because you remind him of himself; where do you want to go to school?" She was a graduate of Coppin State Teachers College in Baltimore, Maryland and I knew that Historically Black Colleges and Universities (HBCU's) were a big thing in her book. I mentioned Morgan State College, but my brothers went there, and I always wanted to take things up a notch, so I said Howard University. Aunt Fanny was not one for showing emotions except for surly, but she managed a half weak smile, which is as good as it got. I knew I had struck a nerve. She said; "Did you know my brother, Dr. Michael Moore wrote a textbook that they use at Howard's Medical School?" I confessed that I didn't. I couldn't share all of my motives for wanting to go to Howard; that it was considered the Black Harvard, that most of the revolutionary Black thinkers had some connection to Howard at one time or that the female to male ratio was rumored to be 7 to 1. There was also something I had forgotten that I said to my mother after a trip to the National Zoo when I was about 7 or 8, that I'm going to live in Washington, DC someday'.

My father was firm. "You didn't want to go to school when you graduated, so you blew your opportunity." Behind the scenes my mother and Aunt Fanny got together and no doubt got help from my father and Uncle Howard and I was off to college for the spring semester 1972.

First day; what a culture shock! I had never been around that many Black people at one time except on our trips to New York. My growing up world had been primarily bi-cultural, white and black. Where I grew up there were no Hispanics and I can't remember any Asians. It was a big deal when one of my older friends would let me ride with him to Baltimore to get Chinese food. I had been up the night before my parents took me to Howard with some of my friends passing the peace pipe and drinking Bali Hai wine. Everything seemed so surreal. The Nation's Capital was bustling on its mortal race and there was Howard University in the center of Sin City. It shone like a safe house in the middle of Sodom and Gomorrah.

My father dropped my mother and I off at the administration building and she and I went and opened up a student account to be able to siphon money to me as needed. We got back in the car and drove the one hundred yards to the front of Cook Hall, my new home away from home. We were met at the door by a Mr. Brown who was the dorm director. He was a very affable man, what we called a confirmed bachelor back in the day. Let the record be straight, he turned out to be one of the most honorable, trustworthy and understanding people I would meet in my new world. My parents were not emotional people and a after a quick handshake and a hug they got back in the car and headed home. Mr. Brown helped with my bags and escorted me to my room and new roommate. David Nixon introduced himself and he was what was considered an older student back then. He was 27 years old. It was immediately evident who was going to be running this camp. He laid out his rules which were; up early, go to class; he went to work in the afternoon, come home to go to dinner in the student cafeteria, come back to the room and study until 9 o'clock. Same routine for 5 days straight. Friday night David would get a 5th of Scotch and sit up until midnight or better, sometimes listening to the radio, which was off limits during week. Saturday morning Richard would wake up groggily around 9 or 10, shower and shave, eat breakfast and after a few hours of drinking copious amounts of water, start studying again. Pretty much he had the same routine on Sunday. David was a shy guy and even though he had an eye for the ladies, he didn't have a clue about getting one. I remember he was carrying a torch for a girl for the whole semester and just when he got his nerve together to ask her out, he found out she was not interested in anything beyond friendship and she was dating one of the campus losers, the kind of guy young women tend to gravitate towards. It truly broke his heart to be turned down and I felt really bad for him.

I owe David a lot. His work ethic rubbed off on me and instead of spending my time gawking at the girls or sitting in some smoke filled room, I developed a brand new concept; studying! First off, I was intimidated for the first time in my life by all of these coeds. I had never been in the company of that many young black beautiful women at one time before in my life. They came from all backgrounds and ran the gamut from poor from Mississippi to lavish from Los Angeles. Tall ones, short ones, from every shade and shape. I was in hog heaven. The intimidation saved me from being a wash-out my first semester. Secondly, since the word of the day back then was narc, short for the pot police, I was blessed with just enough country smarts not to trust people I didn't know. It all added up to a 3.0 GPA at the end of the semester and I felt like I fit in quite nicely. Parents were proud and Aunt Fanny was saying she knew I had it in me all along.

When summer break came along, I told my parents I wanted to stay in DC rather then come home. I got a job through an intern position with the Smithsonian Institute at the National Zoological Park. Since I wasn't going to summer school, I had to move out of the dorm. I got a room in a house on Girard Street with a 99 year old man, named James Pair. Reverend Pair was a graduate of Howard University Class 1903. He and I spent many an hour sitting on his front porch talking about the Howard University and Washington DC in the early 1900's. The house was about twelve blocks from my job and two blocks from campus. It couldn't get any better. To add icing on the cake Rev. Pair had a housekeeper named Ms. Anthy from Jamaica, who not only made my bed, but did my laundry and cooked. I met two guys on the street named Crump and Sanders who had custodial jobs at the zoo and we shared a lot in common; love of women, a little wine and cannabis sativa. These were the ways of the time and these two guys were the good guys. Like me they had a certain moral compass that didn't include anything like stealing, unnecessary fighting or disrespect for older people. I remember several things that happened that summer, but there are a few that stand out in my mind. One time I came home late and flopped down in the bed and went to sleep. The next morning I was running late so I dressed in a hurry and left for work. I had forgotten that I had left a little pile of pot sitting in the middle of the desk in my room. I had taken it out of the bag so I could get all of the seeds out of it. I was in a quandary all day at work and didn't know what to expect when I got home. Rev. Pair who had astigmatism would not have gone in my room anyway, but Ms. Anthy would have gone in to straighten up like always. I greeted Rev. Pair and everything seemed to be as usual. Ms. Anthy had left for the day and it was obvious she hadn't said anything to Rev. Pair. When I went in my room the first thing I noticed is that she had made the bed so I knew she had been in there. I looked over on the desk and Ms. Canty had straightened up my books, put my pens back in their place and lo and behold, she had scraped the pot up in a nice little pile and had it nice and neat on the corner of the desk. She never said a word about it to me. Thank God for Jamaican housekeepers. One other event I remember well is sipping wine in the apartment of a local recording artist. She lived across the street and her apartment became a favorite place to visit on weekends, strictly platonically.

We had some good times that summer, but like everything else, all good things must come to an end. The fall semester was coming around and I wanted to move into a new dorm nicknamed the Penthouse. Carver Hall was located on Elm Street NW, what we later called the "hood". It was a completely refurbished building and everybody who was anybody wanted to live there. Reality has a way of rearing its ugly head and no sooner that I had moved in, I received a letter from the Induction Agency telling me to report to take a physical and pack up to go off to basic training.

The war was winding down and the government decided as a partial way to do away with the draft was to have a lottery based on the date of your birthday. Lower numbers would be inducted and anyone over

275-365 had little or no chance of going. My number was 55 and panic set in. Here I was having the time of my life with my future ahead of me and I was being sucked into a war that I had protested against on many occasions. I can't remember where I got the idea, but I went to the ROTC office and related my story. I was introduced to the head of the department a Colonel Bryant who calmed me down and he took my induction notice and said to get back with him in a couple of days and for 48 hours I didn't sleep. When I went back to see him, he stood up, shook my hand and said welcome to Army ROTC. Apparently he had called some people he knew at the Pentagon and was able to get me a deferment. I was ecstatic, not only could I complete my college; I would be an officer when I graduated and more than likely the war would be over.

Things were moving fast. My neighbor from Bel Air, Maryland and de facto younger brother, Michael Benson Turner was coming in with the new freshman class. We had started elementary school with each other in Bel Air. I was in second grade when he was in first. We walked to school together, played in the band together, played football together, went to the library together and so on and so on. Here we were together again at the Howard Universe. Mike was smart, a little on the naïve puritanical side back then, but he trusted my leadership I guess just because of that one year age difference. I remember two things that come to mind immediately about our friendship; the time when he was in first grade he got his boot caught in the snow and was beside himself. I pulled him and his boot out and you would have thought I had saved him from sharks. When we were in college, he went to see the movie 'The Exorcist' and came back to my dorm room shaking like a leaf. He ended up spending the night sleeping on my dorm room floor. Don't think I'm violating a trust here, he tells these stories as well and if I make 10 cents on this book, he will try to extort 4 cents of it to not tell stories about me. I may have to pay him off.

The fall semester was full of adventure. My buddy was with me, I was in ROTC and coming from a military family was an extra plus in improving my esteem with my family and my home community. Mike and I shared a common goal on planning to attend law school and as kindred ideology in the land of idealism was the making for a perfect storm. As I became more inculcated in university life, I became more comfortable with my fellow students and the residents of the surrounding community. I had a Volkswagen Beatle convertible and a gas credit card that my mother was picking up the tab for and the world was my oyster. Once we rented a Cessna 150 airplane at a local airport through a friend who had his pilot's license. We flew from Clinton, Maryland to an airport on the Eastern Shore of Maryland and back. High times literally. I should have recognized the signs of arrogance seeping in, but like a kid in a candy store you don't realize that you've eaten too much until you are sick. One of the tell tale signs should have been when I went into a liquor store to get a bottle of ceremonial wine for one of our many communions and the owner asked me if I wanted a part-time job. He also said that he would tailor my hours to fit my class schedule. I turned him down. The next two semesters read like a roller coaster. Down in the spring and back up in the fall. I believed I knew how to work the system. Some classes you had to really concentrate on and others you could fudge and get by.

The spring semester of 1974 would be the beginning of the end. I was invited to pledge a fraternity. Since my oldest brother had pledged Alpha Phi Alpha and the frat boys always had the girls, I couldn't say no to the offer. I became an Eternal Sphixman and will be one for eternity. Pledging is a full time job as far as I was concerned and I could not balance school and pledging at the same time. Somewhere in the middle of the pledge period one of my pledge brothers had his nose broken by one of our so-called big brothers. Our fraternity was put on suspension. While the chapter waited for vindication we licked our wounds and tried to regenerate our spirits and our class work. The damage had been done to my semester. I had either withdrawn or failed all of my classes. I was totally disillusioned by the whole process. I tried unsuccessfully to resurrect my career in a summer session, but my parents had lost faith in my commitment and so had I. My associations in the neighborhood were pulling me harder than school. Making money was my new thing and I began to hustle, which is a subject for a whole different book. The point is my college days of the 70's were over.

Chapter 3
What Happened In the Intervening Years...

In the fall of 1974, I hung around the DC area living in an apartment that Mike and I shared, but by not being a student I felt self conscious about showing my face on campus. Since most of my friends were in school, I went up on campus to hang out and I lived the policy of don't ask, don't tell, so most of the students didn't know I was not enrolled. I even had the audacity to go to some of the homecoming events, but the lie was catching up to me. By the spring of 1975, our apartment arrangement had dissolved because I was out of work and had no help from home. With a mother's undeserved kindness, my mother arranged to have me shipped off to her sister's house in Richmond, Virginia. This was my first encounter with depression and try as I might, I couldn't shake that fact that I had failed. My Aunt was a no nonsense person and everyday I heard her say I had to get a job. My Uncle had some connections at the Virginia State Penitentiary, 100 Spring Street, maximum security, so I got a job as a correctional officer. I was managing to keep my libido exercised and there was plenty of underground nightlife. My future cousin-in-law was a who's who in Richmond let me hang out with him and hanging out with him was always a good time. Things went south with me staying with my relatives so I moved into a rooming house on the edge of the Virginia Commonwealth University campus. I hit it off with a couple of VCU coeds and was able to maintain my insatiable appetite for female companionship. By the summer of 1975, I had begged my mother to come rescue me and get me back to DC. Now I had a taste for money and I made that my priority. I was able to get a room in the house of a distant relative about 6 blocks from Howard and got a job at a liquor store in one of the roughest neighborhoods in DC. In addition to being a clerk, we, the employees supplied most of the boot leg houses with cut rate liquor for sales after hours. The money was good. We had two or three hustles going on at the same time. Since I was a good old honest clean cut country boy, I was asked to take illegal number slips to what is known as the banker, because the cops thought I was Joe College and they did not give me a lot of notice. Like I said the money was good, the risks were minimal and the street status was incalculable. This is a story for another book.

Falling in love for the millionth time, I met a girl who made me want to think about the future. I left the liquor store even though the owner wanted me to be his heir apparent. I got a job at United Mine Workers, Health and Retirement Fund at 2021 "K" St, NW, the heart and soul of Washington government corruption. The major players wore Brooks Brother suits. I liked the step up on the social scale, but soon realized that I wanted something more, plus most of my peers were college graduates. I fit in easily because I've always been a big reader and what I lacked in classroom time I over compensated in book and street knowledge. I easily maintained credibility as a young professional and through the years I have been mistaken for doctors several times as well as a lawyer. I usually ask people; "Do I have that slippery look about me?" (That's a rhetorical question!)The girl that had changed my mind turned out to be incompatible with me and I drifted from date to date while licking my wounds.

I went to work for a company named M.S. Ginn that sold office supplies to most of the big offices in the Washington area. I met a girl who later became my wife and we worked together. We left that company together to take jobs with a competitor and after a year of living together and a year and a half of marriage, the whole thing came unglued. I was devastated, because I had the old fashion belief that divorce is not an option. The company had tried to expand too fast and with a marriage on the skids, the company and I went out of business.

I got a job with Jordan Kitts Music, a piano and organ company partly because I could play few ditties and I didn't mind looking like a fool standing in the entrance of the store in a mall playing just enough to entice people to want to come in and buy something that most will probably rarely use. Little did I know that the woman I would eventually marry and be the mother of my kids was working two stores away at Sears? Our paths didn't cross until later, but ain't life funny.

I met a minister through calling around for counseling, because I was still bugging about my marital break up. This guy comes to my job and prays with me and then reaches in his pocket and pulls out a twenty dollar bill and said God told him to give it to me. I needed that twenty because I was broke and driving around on vapors. He invited me to his church and it turned out to be a school building that he was trying to covert into a church. There were ten people sitting on folding chairs he had set up. Pastor Bob Whitaker turned out to be a friend and brother. I was unable to keep the apartment that my ex-wife and I had lived in and Bob asked me to come and live with his family. He had a beautiful wife named Sandy, who agreed to let me live with them and their three young sons. Bob was committed to making his church a success and as time went on the congregation grew. One of the co-founders of the church was a Howard grad as was Bob. As he struggled to pay the huge rent and later huge mortgage, I got the bright idea to start a day care center in the building; after all it was a former school. I became the headmaster and with volunteer help from a couple of the women in the church we took in enough kids to pay the bills and get a few converts in the process.

I married my wife Carol on October 22nd, 1983. In my prayers I must have put in all the ingredients I wanted in a wife and got just what I prayed for. We had our first child a daughter, named Natalie in 1985 and a son Nelson Jr. in 1986. My wife supported my decision to go into the Army at age 33 and during our separation while I was stationed in Germany she opted to move near my parents even though I gave her choices for other places. She was the consummate mother. Our children were reading by ages 3 and 4, she read to them, played games with them and made sure they had a healthy diet. I became the President of the PTA at their elementary school, Vice-President at their middle school and their substitute teacher when they were in high school. When my daughter started her first day at Howard University, I walked her to her first class. When my son went to Basic Training, I drove him to the recruiter's office even though they would have picked him up at home. Before I did these things I discussed it with them first. They have never seemed to be intimidated or embarrassed by me or their mother. It helped that their friends thought we were cool (sometimes). Even though my son joined the Army after high school and I was proud of him, I cursed myself for making it sound too glamorous. He went to jump school and became a member of the 82nd Airborne. On his third qualification jump from a C-130 he jokingly told his mother he would call her on his cell phone while he was parachuting to the ground, at least I hoped it was a joke. He was in combat in Afghanistan and Iraq. I died everyday he was there. For me to go back to school in their eyes is almost normal. All of my family thinks status quo sucks. We have a policy of keeping it real and from the time they were very young up to now, we don't color the truth. Santa Claus, the Easter Bunny and definitely Halloween were talked about truthfully, hopefully demystifying the hype. Living a lie does not do a child any better than it does an adult or maybe worse. We create enough fantasies in our minds without adding external ones. Both of our kids turned out to be smart productive citizens without the fantasy. So Virginia, I don't know what to tell you about Santa Claus. (You might have to explain that one to people under 50.)

In the intervening years, I had worked in a myriad of jobs always seeking something better. I was in the Army for 6 years on active duty with a little less than 2 years in Germany away from my family. When I left the Army I became a Test Director as a contractor with the Department of Defense. I was traveling to government test sites for at least one week a month to places like Arizona, Texas and California. My wife carried the torch to keep the home fires operating efficiently.

During the years preceding going back to school, I managed a Medicaid qualification company and was selected to serve on the Disability Commission for Montgomery County, Maryland, which advocates for the disabled. For two years I served as its chairman. Prior to that I was on the Ethics Committee in the Town of Bel Air, Maryland. I served as a CASA, Court Appointed Special Advocate for children placed in foster care which prepares case files for presentation before judges in custody hearings. I have held licenses as a real estate agent and currently hold licenses for life and health insurances. In addition to a business license to conduct business with social services, I have received several designations to contract business by bid and solicitation with the county, state and federal government. My company, NJAX Unlimited is on the verge of taking on some new big projects. Now my days, all seven of them, require hours of study to complete the degree I did not get in the 70's in conjunction with making a business perform to maximum efficiency. I love every minute of it.

Chapter 4
The View on the Campus

On just about any college campus in America, I'm sure you will see some of the most enticing young men or women in one location that you may ever encounter. Most are not only cute, but they are smart as well. Since they are in a university setting, they are full of ideology, optimism and unabashed curiosity. Before you even think about returning to school you may need to do some self examination and honestly ask yourself; do I possess the integrity and discipline to behave as an adult in the middle of all this temptation? If you have a moment's doubt, take on-line courses and stay off of a campus. If you can't behave as you would around your wife or husband and your children, stay home. As an illustration of the naivety and insensitivity of our fellow human beings, when I was a substitute teacher at a local high school a relative (male) asked me if I hit on any of the hot girls in my classes? To make a long story short, I haven't spoken to him since. Bottom line your first test is to ask yourself if you have integrity even when no one is watching.

I laugh every time I hear the debate about "don't ask, don't tell" military policy as it applied to homosexuals. It was always the heterosexuals who were the most disgusting, rude and obnoxious in my unit and similarly you will see this behavior on a college campus. A lot of young men tend to think like sexist pigs and think women are to be treated as sex objects. My experience in the Army Infantry is you don't have time to worry about how the next guy or girl gets it on in his or her private time the same should be true in college. When I was in the Army we were too tired from training to think about a person's sexual proclivities. On weekend's people tended to gravitate to like-minded people as they do in any other place. In a lot of instances black soldiers hung out with other black soldiers and white soldiers tended to hang out with other white soldiers There is a lot of positive integration within units, because you have been trained to think of each other as your brothers and sisters. Guys that liked to play video games hung out together, black, white, brown, yellow together. Soldiers that liked to read headed for the library. Come Monday morning everybody was green all over again. The point is this; sexually of any kind can not be issue for any returning older student. If you haven't matured to a level to understand that, perhaps you need remedial upbringing. The same goes if you are some religious zealot. Leave it at home. This is academia, a place to discuss ideas and share opinions, not a Baptist pulpit. As a Christian I fully understand that I cannot and will not deny my faith, but unless someone wants to share that with me outside of the classroom, my opinion is personal. By the same token if you have some business or sideline that you are pursuing, you would be wise to leave that as home as well. Remember, the people you probably hate the most are the ones that sell raffle tickets. Basically, come as an empty vessel and allow yourself to be filled.

When I was here in the 70's, at least 99% of all students hated the Viet Nam War. Almost every student had some experience of having been overtly discriminated against more than once. Bell bottoms were in as were platform shoes. R & B music ruled the house parties, but jazz was the music of the cool and intellectual. The songs of the Temptations and Four Tops was what you listened to back home, but the minute you set foot on campus, it was John Coltrane and Miles Davis. Little has changed 30 years later. The easy listening music we play on the car radio gives way to Gangsta Rap, Hip Hop and what I call new wave Rock and Roll. The generations are miles apart in music appreciation. Don't pass judgement! Listen and learn and you can get a sense of where and what the thinking is of the people who will be the new ruling class. They are our leaders of tomorrow. Climb on and jump in because this train is not coming back. You don't have to like it, but you will do well to try to understand it.

Look around yourself! If you are lucky enough to be on a campus constructed over 100 years ago, you will do well to know some of the history of the place. On Howard's campus there are buildings like Douglass Hall, named after the abolitionist Frederick Douglass. Most of the student's do not know that he was also a trustee at Howard. The building itself was designed by an African-American architect named Albert Cassell. Because of your age, the younger students will expect that you know that and can answer questions about it when asked. If you are in the mood to "flip the script" sometimes ask one of them do they know its history. Be careful, you might get an answer like the reason you know it is because you were there when it was built. After all these years I am still learning about the history of our colleges. Most people don't know that Howard University was commissioned to be founded by a white man and Georgetown University by a black Jesuit priest. Go figure!

Locke Hall, named after Alain Locke, a former educator and the founder of the philosophy department. The Harlem Renaissance, which America enjoys the fruit of today was in large part initiated by Locke. The world would be a much different place without his contribution to society.

Founders Library, named for the seventeen founders of the university. This iconic building symbolizes learning and academia and its architecture is represented on most of the great universities as the centerpiece of higher education.

Do your homework before you get on the campus about a school's history, so you are not walking around like a "Gump" (someone who looks confused, like a tourist from Shanghai in Manhattan). If you unfamiliar with a campus, spend some time orientating yourself to where your classes are. You might want to time yourself and walk the distance between classes in a dress rehearsal. A few minutes difference can be crucial and if you covet certain seats like I do, you better get there first. There is no old folk's courtesy when it comes to seating. Everybody's tuition is equal as well it should be.

Just as important as knowing where your classes are located is making sure that you know where your course offices are and where your course advisor is located. It is important that you meet with your professors at least once during the semester outside of the classroom. Don't go in trying to be folksy. Treat it as any other professional encounter you might have. They are like the employer and you are the employee. Use all of the rules you've learned in business when dealing with someone above your pay grade. For example, don't commiserate. Professors don't have time nor do they care that the car broke down, your daughter has to get braces or you're late for a veterinarian appointment. If you happen to see them in a restaurant or a bar after hours, its okay to be a little more casual as long as you know how to cut it off come class time. Sharing a lot of personal information will only come back to haunt you and you will give all of us returnees a bad reputation. Even professors are looking for signs that you might be over your head with responsibilities. One professor made it perfectly clear; "while you are here, this is your job!"

If you like food like me, you want to scout out the good eating places close by to your classes. You might want to categorize them by price, time and location. I purchased a couple of lunches and had no time to eat them even though some professors didn't mind eating in class. I find that to be rude. That's the old school in me.

Male or female when you get around or above fifty, you need to know where the bathrooms are located. Where the clean ones are and where you can have a peaceful sit down if necessary. I'll let your mind finish this paragraph.

Get to know your library. When I'm concentrating, I like quiet and few distractions. During the warmer days I did on occasion sit on the main campus to people watch while studying. It may have cost me a "B" and I ended up with a "C" on one exam.

Get to know where the available parking locations are in proximity to your classes. I have been on a hundred college campus's at one time or another and I always had issues with parking. On an urban campus like Howard multiply those problems by ten. Any DC resident will tell you, the meter maggots (I say that with caution, I hope they don't read this book) will have a boot put on your car if you have unpaid parking tickets. Public transportation has its issues as well. The Washington Metropolitan Area Transit Authority, WMATA, ("wah, mah, ta" as it is affectionately known, it should be called "wah, wah, wah"), is probably one of the newest rail transit systems in the country and probably one of the poorest run (this time I don't care if they read the book). I can only pray that some Howard graduate will someday take it over.

Finally, one thing that I noticed on the campus of 2010 different from the 70's is that I may have seen 2 or 3 students smoking cigarettes on campus the entire semester. There is no smoking ban on the campus that I know about; this is just a generation that seems to recognize that smoking is detrimental to your health and definitly not cool. When I came to school in 1972, smoking was allowed in the classrooms. We've come a long way baby! This is another of the many reasons I love these guys, they are living proof of evolution and hope for our future.

Chapter 5
Student Reaction: The Perception vs. Reality

Imagine that you've been asked to prepare for a trip to somewhere you have been before 30 plus years ago. Periodically you may have driven through or flown over, you may have even stopped for a brief visit on occasion. One of your children may have lived there in the recent past and knew the layout better than you remember it. The people you used to know are probably no longer there. Things have changed. That's the way I felt in the weeks and days leading up to me returning to campus. In fact I searched my email everyday expecting the offer to be rescinded. It was like planning for a ride in the space shuttle. It's all fun and games until you hear the explosion of the rockets.

More than doing the work and being able to keep up, more than juggling family obligations and more than the opinions of outsiders, the number one anxiety that I felt prior to the first day was what will my fellow classmates would think of me. I would be the outsider or the interloper. The persons who will be my classmates are no longer young people, kids, young adults or just any old students; these people are going to be my peers. I have belonged to lot of organizations over the years, the Army is one of the best training grounds to learn how to adapt and overcome, but this task had a gravitas with dozens of contingencies attached to it. Failure is not an option.

I had over the years visited Howard's campus for one reason or another and even ate my lunch on campus during warm days when I was on the road with my job. One day I didn't have anything better to do so after I ate my lunch, I went around campus and picked up litter that had been dropped or thrown down. The campus was hosting a group of high school kids and they had forgotten their home training and left paper and plastic bottles all over the "yard". I made sure they saw me picking it up. Some got the message and some did not. In that instance I was operating as a parent, teacher or person in authority of some kind. All that being said, as a student, I am still going to be ecologically active, but with my peers unlike the high school students, this is just what I do, not a lesson. It may look the same, just picking up paper, but the projection of my attitude will be totally different. I have a vested interest in this campus as do my peers and no one person is greater than the other. You will know the difference, the minute they take your picture and they give you a student ID card. When I was in the Army and was promoted from a lower enlisted rank to a Non-Commissioned Officer, a friend of mine who was a First Sergeant told me that I would change the minute those bars were pinned on me. He was right. It may have been my mind playing tricks on me, but I felt everyone looked at me differently. That's the same feeling I got when I became a student again, not a parent, not a husband, not a businessman or anything else I had achieved over the years. The playing field had been leveled.

No one likes to be rejected, I don't care how much smoke they blow up your anus and say it ain't so. The power of the tongue is biblically spoken of as having power beyond imagination and it possesses the power to breathe negative life by the perception of rejection. Rejection with or without any spoken word can bring a strong man to his knees. Rejection by a parent has been linked to most of the serial criminals. Anyone who undertakes a job that will take him or her out of their natural age group, be it teacher, student, boy or girl scout master knows that success or failure will hinge on perceptions of rejection or inclusion. When I was in first grade I was a lonely black kid in a sea of white kids, I didn't understand rejection or inclusion like I do today, but I sure knew life got better when the other kids started to play with me.

My first day of classes, I had worn a suit and tie because I had business to take care of after I left the campus. When I sat down in my first class, basically everybody was looking around at everybody and not at me. I forgot to factor in that I was not the only new kid on the block. Most of these students did not know each other. There I sat worrying about fitting in with them and they were probably much more concerned about how they would fit in with each other.

Basically the reaction from the students was largely ambivalence. When the first class was over, everybody got up from their seats and headed for the next class. I was relieved as well as shocked, because in my mind I had made up all of these scenarios where at least some students would come up to me to get my story. It didn't happen. The students conducted themselves even more professionally than many of my peers in business. I understood better later when a student approached me towards the end on the semester to ask me if I had an idea what I thought we needed to study for the final exam. We talked briefly and somehow the conversation came by my initiation that I was here because I didn't apply myself when I was here as a young man. I liked to make the joke that when I was in school before it was my parent's money, this time it was my money. The young man opened up and said that he had to study as hard as he could because he and his mother both worked hard to be able to get him in to college and he was not going to let her down. That was another of those moments that made this whole experience more than worth it. I made sure that I gave him my detailed notes to copy and I gave him my email address, because if ever a person deserved all of the support he can get, he was it.

It was a student, Khyrie Alleyne that gave me the inspiration for the book. We had been in class for about three weeks when this guy sat down beside me. He used to ask me to save him a seat and he told me that he had been home to New York over the previous weekend last winter and he had told his mother about me. He told her that he wanted her to go back to school, because he saw me doing it. It doesn't get any better than that. I told him jokingly that I ought to write a book and he looked at me very seriously and said; "you should"! Needless to say, he and I are still friends and continue to share some classes.

In another class a guy sat down beside me and gave me a compliment on my sport jacket. I always noticed that he always came to class with the preppy look I was familiar with from private school. Unlike a lot of his peers, he generally wore nice slacks and tie to class. He told me that he taught himself that how he is perceived is very important to him. He recognized that you can get more credibility by maintaining a neat appearance more so than wearing pants hung down half way off your butt. I just listened in awe. He shared with me that he had family members who were incarcerated and one sibling who was killed. He is determined to break the cycle, so much so that he doesn't just want to be a teacher; he wants to start an academy for at risk kids. And you wonder why I couldn't wait to go to school each day! People like him are living inspirations.

I shied away from non academic activities for two reasons; one, I had to try to make a living for some hours of each day and two; unless my wife or daughter attended with me I felt it inappropriate for that level of fraternization. I love music like the best of them. I own a Fender bass guitar and a Yamaha electric piano. It's a clarion call for me to want to go to some of the music events on campus, that's not exactly what I mean. Like Justice John Potter Stewart said on the Supreme Court, and I'm paraphrasing, "I can't define pornography, but I know it when I see it." That's the way I feel about over fraternization. Your moral compass should warn you when you are getting too close to the flames. I have received emails from students requesting information on class assignments, no problem. I have walked from one class to another with female students, no problem. What I'm not going to do is go into some student's dorm room, male or female. I would have little problem giving students, multiple riders preferred, a ride if needed, but they won't be hanging out with me to go anywhere. Nelson's Law!

In my poetry class, we had an assignment to prepare a poetry reading in groups of 5 or 6, and the final product was to be presented somewhere else other than the classroom. One group had theirs in a locally owned bookstore, whereas most of the rest of us held ours outside because spring had sprung. It felt good to be asked to be included in one of the groups and not have to fish around to ask to be included. There were some students that didn't get picked right away. We had a poetry reading at the same bookstore on another occasion and the professor asked me to be the emcee. Another, I'm one of the guys feeling.

All was not peaches and cream. The one class I felt somewhat uncomfortable in, I had more than one Alka Seltzer moment. In addition to the feeling that the professor was looking to hijack me, he brought up a subject for discussion about whether the students felt comfortable with their parents or older people partying at a club for young people. I was surprised because several of the students said they wouldn't like it. One student even went far enough to say that old folks need to stay in their place. I laughed at this because at first I didn't think he was serious, but when I raised my hand to offer rebuttal, this professor refused to call on me. Since I was the only old guy in class, I would have thought that they wanted to hear another side, but there was something sinister in the motives of that professor and I was disappointed.

Attitude is everything and if you have some altruistic agenda other than completing your goal, understand this; the students are observing your actions and attitude daily. They learn from you just as much as you learn from them. Don't ruin the attitude of these young people by bringing a stale funky attitude to the classroom. In my overall evaluation, I have to say that the girls were friendlier than the boys, in the sense that they were generally the first ones to speak or say hello and were generally the most helpful when I had questions about where or how things were done. I was however surprised at the friendliness of some of the guys, because I didn't expect it. Men even in professional meetings tend to very territorial. My interaction with the students I believe to have been just right. Not too hot and not too cold.

Chapter 6
Reaction to and from the Professors…

I happen to be a people person. Collectively I generally like people, I like watching them, talking with them, and learning from them; the good and the bad. Some of us are not people persons. My wife is not a people person, she is cautious about precipitous friendships and she is wary of motives. She is not easily fooled, but her reticence can sometimes mistake innocence for vindictiveness. We compliment each other in that regard. It reminds me of a western movie I like, where the main character gets fooled by a woman and gets robbed and pushed down in a hole after she tells him that there is a two headed varmint in it and he just has to see it. When he gets out of the hole and meets his romantic interest she tries to get him to commit to a relationship; he says that he's the kind of guy that's always looking for a varmint and it always gets him into trouble. I can't count the number of times I've made mistakes in judging character. By the grace of God none have hurt me irreparably; but some have left me with deep emotional scars.

There was little about going back to school and interacting with the professors or the administrators that made me nervous. I have chaired commissions, testified before government officials and briefed military officers in the top ranks. I remember one time I gave a speech as the President of a local PTA to a bunch of elementary school kids. That was the one time I felt nervous because kids can see right through you and if you are disingenuous you might as well wear a kick me sign on your face. I don't want to come off as arrogant but based on my life experiences I felt I was on par with the university staff. Where I do have a modicum of wisdom was to understand unequivocally that they had something that I wanted; the roadmap to graduation. I will always remember a time when I was in the Army and a soldier with the rank of major was too proud to ask a private how a certain thing was done and his pride cost him his dignity and probably a promotion.

Howard University just like most colleges and universities; have assembled some of the best minds and devoted educators that they can find to enrich the minds of those that want it. It is fascinating to watch a person that through discipline has made themselves into subject matter experts. There is a difference in studying something for a semester and studying something for 8, 10 or 12 years. If you think you have as much knowledge as that person already, you have no need to go back to school. You are ready to teach. To get a degree is to have that knowledge certified and to acknowledge that the certification has personal value.

There are always personality differences especially among adults. The older you get the less likely that you want to be told what or how to do anything. Examine your personality before you write that check, because that is what is going to happen every weekday for 4 or 5 months. If you're married and/or have kids than there is no vacation or weekends from being told what you should do by them. Imagine yourself being instructed by a person half your age with as many degrees as Einstein and dresses and wears his or her hair unlike your model of what a professor should look like. On today's campuses you won't find many professors that wear tweed jackets and wing tip shoes. If you have been successful in your previous life and are used to giving orders more than taking them, you need to self assess.

Because I am a people person, I liked the adventure of sorting through the maze of personalities and using my people skills to adapt.

Former students returning (FSR"s) don't have the luxury or the time of choosing professors because you've heard that he or she is a great, funny or entertaining person. The goal for us is complete a mission. I don't care about the personalities, but I must confess that some of the stress can be diminished if you have a warm and empathetic instructor. It is much easier to handle the three pronged battle; school, home and job, if the professor is stimulating as well as likable. Just keep in mind that it won't always be that way and just like on a job you just have to remain focused on your goal. Remind yourself that you're not there to make friends. When you do make friends then consider it as a happy by-product. It will happen between you and some of your professors, but maintain that same professionalism you would use on a job. Over fraternization is not an option. It will backfire on you. Don't think for one minute that because of your age you are entitled to some special dispensation. If you can't compete fairly without benefit of age affirmative action, then take on-line courses.

Basically I like the professors that I have been in direct contact with, because as in true academia they encourage differences of opinion. If fact if you are a yes man or yes lady you add nothing of value to the education experience. When in class you have an opportunity to offer a different perspective to the discussion, just don't couch your opinion with old age paternalism. You are not smarter; just offering a different perspective. The student from Bangladesh is offering a different perspective as well. The difference is he or she is not using age as a measure of intelligent quotient.

Previously I made a comment in this book that could be conceived by some as being sexist, when I said my Spanish professor was an attractive Latino lady. I'm not going to take it back, but I will put it into context. This is real life, to deny that she has a good command of the students attention would be a lie. The students seemed to like her, male and female, because she maintains her position of authority. Let's be real, that innate desire of males particularly is to want to show the nice lady how smart we are. Yes older students will be judged differently than younger students. It is an unspoken rule, but you will recognize the differences as easily as black, Asian or Hispanics recognize different treatment based on their race or for that matter the way women can recognize sexism.

One of my male political science professors captivates his audience by the depth of his knowledge and his satirical humor. You want to be in his class. You will learn something. You will get your money's worth. One of my female political science professors is a classic interrogator and would have made a good attorney. Through a series of questions she gets inside of your head and she doesn't have to critique your answers, you'll do that all by yourself.

I was amazed how easily that these professors accepted me as just another student in their class. It was extremely helpful to my learning experience that I could blend in. My daughter had told me before I started, to get over it; "Dad you're not the first old geezer that these guys have taught (It's the "g" word; she's allowed to say it, not you.) They are probably happy that you come to class on time and don't play with your cell phone." Which brings up another subject that we shouldn't have to discuss; don't think because you have a lot going on in your life that you have to take that phone call or return that email as if the president is trying to contact you. There were a lot of students in my classes that I would have thrown out if I was in charge who play with their phones and laptops. Schools need the same zapper system that most hospitals have to disable the devices when you're in certain spots. Be thankful I'm not the professor. I applaud the professor's patience and composure.

One of my professors had no fear of criticizing students on their dress styles or overall personal appearance. He did it creatively and was not offensive, but the message was clear and I for one thought it was healthy part of the educational process. I had to think back to when I was in college in the 70's and how in trying to find myself I dressed like a clown on occasion. My peers and a couple of girlfriends cured me over time.

Like moving into any community, after time people not only accept you, they start to look for your appearance every day. If you are sick or go away for a time, people will notice. You become inculcated into a family of sorts. Professor's share experiences about their personal lives with students and the concerns are reciprocated. In no cases can I say that I was talked down to or did I witness other students being treated condescendingly. I did hear of conflicts from some students with professors and I think that's natural. Part of the learning process for the young and old is to learn how to resolve conflicts. I confess that when I heard stories about conflicts with students and the administration, the parent in me kicks in. My daughter had her own share of easily solvable problems, which could have ruined her entire undergraduate experience if not for my intervention. I can only imagine what a student must be going through when there is no parent or guardian there to help them. Conversely as a former student returning, I needed the help of my young peers on many occasion and I'm not too proud to ask for their help.

A bonus that age has on campus is that most of the staff relates to you as a social equal when it comes to engaging in conversation. Periodically it is forgotten that you are a student and you can be mistaken for staff. Wisdom dictates that you keep it in perspective and don't wait until a staff member has to get you back into your place. The reason you are there should be repeated silently to yourself everyday, just like a prayer.

Chapter 7
Interaction with the Administration

The mere word "administration" should scare the hell out of anybody who has ever come face-to-face with one. The dictionary defines "administration" as:

ad·min·is·tra·tion

Show Spelled [ad-min-uh-strey-shuh-n] Show IPA
—noun
1.
the management of any office, business, or organization; direction.
2.
the function of a political state in exercising its governmental duties.
3.
the duty or duties of an administrator in exercising the executive functions of the position.
4.
the management by an administrator of such duties.
5.
a body of administrators, esp. in government.

6.
(often initial capital letter) the executive branch of the U.S. government as headed by the President and in power during his or her term of office: The Administration has threatened to veto the new bill. The Reagan administration followed President Carter's.

7.
the period of service of a governmental administrator or body of governmental administrators.

8.
any group entrusted with executive or administrative powers: the administration of a college.

9.
Law. management of a decedent's estate by an executor or administrator, or of a trust estate by a trustee.

10.
an act of dispensing, esp. formally: administration of the sacraments.

11.
supervision of the taking of an oath or the like.

12.
application, as of a salve or medicine.

Use administration in a sentence
See images of administration
Search administration on the web

Origin:
1275–1325; ME administracio (u) n < L administrātiōn- (s. of administrātiō) service. See administra-tion

Dictionary.com Unabridged

Based on the Random House Dictionary, © Random House, Inc. 2010.

Let's dissect the definitions the way a university administration works:

Item 1: Management of an office…organization. *Let the cartoons begin. To administrate and manage should probably be never used in the same sentence. On a college or university you have a brain trust of competing ego's and territorial eccentrics that make the problems of the CIA and FBI not communicating with each other elementary in comparison.*

Item 2: *Function does not always imply that something is working efficiently. My car functions, but it has never seen a mechanic it didn't like.*

Item 3: Duties of..... *For administrators to make sure that they are sufficiently unavailable when needed.*

Item 4: Management of duties.... *Ensure that I get all my points on my Starbucks Reward Card,*

Item 5: Administrate and government. *It hurts to even write this one.*

Item 6: To describe how the Executive Branch operates, *I'll let you make your own jokes.*

Item 7: The period of service..... *I will stay as long as they let me or until they catch on.*

Item 8: Entrusted with power.....*Look for the fine print that tells you how to revoke that power.*

Item 9: Law management....*Create ways to make cookie cutter solutions to correct human conditions.*

Item 10: Administration of sacraments.....*The only definition that acknowledges we need prayer.*

Item 11: Supervision...... *an administrator doesn't supervise, he or she delegates to someone else to do the dirty work.*

Item 12: Application of a salve or medicine.... *Let us all pray and take an aspirin.*

Do you detect a certain cynicism in my opinion of administrators and administrations? I have made a business of trying to negotiate bureaucracies. I have had people argue with me that all a person has to do is follow the directions and stand in a line and everything will be alright. Basically they say that you don't need a facilitator or an advocate. If you're older than 12 years you know better than that. One of the top lawyers in the State of Maryland recently told me that when he tried to get social services help for one of his relatives, he realized he was in way over his head. Being book smart is not a requisite to getting something accomplished through an administration. You need to have blind, dogged determination and the ability to act totally mentally challenged to ignore the stupid instructions of administrations.

At the end of the semester, I heard students say that won't graduate on time because their shot records were not updated or their final closing payment came two days after the deadline. Cookie cutter solutions to easily solvable problems and they wonder why people have problems donating to endowments. My daughter was on the on the dean's list for the entire 4 years she was in undergraduate school. One month before graduation she was notified that she owed roughly 12 hundred dollars in payment if fees. My wife and I were struggling with a myriad of obligations, not to mention some sort of celebration to mark my daughter's accomplishment. It was not the amount of money, it was the timeliness that required we go back and jiggle our resources. We past the deadline by two days. I started calling the administrators and if I wasn't put on hold, I was promised a return phone call that never came. I took off from work and came to the university to meet with a top administrator who will go nameless. We sat in his expansive office where he puffed up bigger than a blowfish. In the end he acknowledged that he had the power to fix the problem and after a bunch of toothy smiles and handshakes he left my daughter and I with the impression that everything would be fixed. He even congratulated my daughter on achieving "cum laude" status. So we thought, back to celebration planning! Talk about premature ejaculation; two days later I got a message from his secretary to say that he had decided that he must stand on policy and she would not be able to graduate with her class. Little did he know that I pride myself on eating administrators for breakfast. My motto is, "even if I lose there will be two beat up bodies left lying on the ground, mine and theirs." I called in a few favors with some senators I know. I threatened to contact some friends on the Washington Post newspaper. I called every administrator who would take my call. I left voice messages, I talked to secretaries and I considered enlisting students to threaten a sit-in. When I requested a meeting with the dean of the school, I received a phone call from the assistant dean. She over-ruled the Howdy Dowdy decision of the other administrator. My daughter graduated with her class!

Lesson for us former students returning; I don't care what college or university you attend, you are going to run into double speak, obfuscation and out right sloppy administration. If you ain't up to the task, take your ball and bat and go home.

There is a whole different side to the administration maze and personnel that must be told. I met some of the most awesome people you may ever want to meet that helped me transition back into school. I was getting the run around going back and forth from building to building to get officially re-enrolled. At every stop I got different information. Finally I ended up in the Admissions office and after finally getting the gatekeeper to understand what I needed; she referred me to the Associate Director of Admissions by the name of Mrs. Tammy I. McCants. Every school needs one. She took me back to her office and had me sit down while she personally looked in her computer to identify the problem and make corrections. Ordinarily what she did would have been delegated. Since the changes could not all take place immediately, she gave me her business card, which contained all of her contact information and promised to correct the problems. To allay my anxieties, she told me to stay in touch by email and/or phone. Call her direct line, what a novel concept. When I left I was doubtful to say the least. I was afraid this was a way to get me out of her office and I would be forgotten within 15 minutes. Boy was I wrong! I emailed her about 4 days later and she replied almost immediately. I went by her office the next week and she remembered me and again brought me back to her office where she made the final corrections. Once again she could have delegated those responsibilities, but she didn't. After that everything went just as she promised. For the entire semester I wanted to go by her office and take her a dozen roses, but every time I stopped in just to say hello, she was busy helping other students and I wasn't going to get in the way of that. Our paths will cross again, that's my promise. Truly if it had not been for her, I would have regretted my decision to go back to school. I have made money over the years exceeding the levels of a lot of college graduates and I didn't need the aggravation, but this was something in my gut I felt I needed to do. She was my confirmation that my decision was right.

To highlight the fact that there are many others that are immaculately professional I have to mention a few. In the School of Arts and Sciences there are a group of ladies that I almost feel like family with. They help and chide, whatever it takes, but they get the job done. I met the director of that department as well and it's easy to see that it is her leadership that inspires that office. The head of the English department, who is a lady younger than me that exhibits wisdom as well as sound administration and wears it well. I met a lady in the Finances office who I believe was in charge, if she is not she should be, because she patiently answered all of my questions and once again gave me her direct line phone number. I met the dean of the Political Science department who to this day remembers our meeting and acknowledges me when ever he sees me. You might not think that it's such a big deal, but it is to me. I thank all of them for that little bit of personal attention and many others like them.

Another example of administrative shortcomings that can be easily overcome is the use of electronic communication to facilitate enrollment, admission and graduation and is a good segue to the next chapter.

Chapter 8
Negotiating College in the Electronic Age

Gadgets create more gimmicks. The more we try to simplify a thing, the more complex it becomes. Take note of a mechanic or plumber who comes on a job with a big box of tools, he or she is destined to create as many problems as get fixed. Its human nature to use everything you carry even if it's unnecessary, ask a hiker or better still ask a soldier. Computers and cell phones are no different. For example, if a cell phone's purpose is to send and receive calls, why do they keep adding more and more applications to distract you. The object is to get you so engrossed in wasting time that you accumulate exorbitant bills. Don't be hoodwinked. Americans want more and more gizmos on their cars and 75% of people can't drive a car with the radio on. I don't know if things have changed, but traditionally Italian sport cars were made for one thing; driving! They recognized that to do it well requires all of your concentration. Use your gadgets at school for the purpose they were intended, no more and no less.

The other side of the equation is that we have so much of technology that we don't have time to learn to use it to its full capacity and efficiency. If you are not at least basic technology literate, you might want to consider taking lessons from your kids and grand kids before getting started. They know everything; just don't let them get you further confused by teaching you things that you don't need to know. An example is, you don't need to know how to download music on a MP3 player. You will however need to know how to send and receive email and use the internet. I don't know many people who can't do that by now, but you never know. If you don't already know, learn how to put your cell phone on vibrate or turn it off. Once you've mastered these two things you have successfully completed the things you will definitely need. Congratulations you have just completed remedial re-entry class 101. All other tricks that you need to know can be achieved by asking a fellow student. This is your opportunity to make a friend.

Even though laptops are allowed in the classrooms and probably encouraged in some, I like the old-fashioned pen and paper method of note taking. My rational is that when I go back home at the end of the day, I put my notes on my computer and that guarantees that I will have looked at my notes at least twice in the same day. You will notice laptop users looking at soap operas or hopefully not x-rated material in class. The professors must have taken an oath not to commit homicide, because if I was in charge, I would go ballistic.

Even the young genii don't make proper application of their gadgets. My Spanish professor makes use of an application by the university called a blackboard where you can post individual or group messages. The first thing I do when I get up in the morning is check my emails for school and business. One morning I had a message to check the blackboard. The Spanish professor wrote that class would be cancelled that day due to a prior commitment. I had another class at a time before Spanish so I had to go on campus anyway. For the sake of caution, I went to the Spanish class just to be sure; after all I was already on campus. When I got there thirty students sat waiting patiently for the professor. I announced that the professor had posted a message that she would not be in class that day and I almost got ran over by the stampeding exodus. I waited around for a while just in case I was wrong. One other cautious student stayed with me. I couldn't believe that all of those computer experts had not bothered to access the application that was set up for that very purpose. Score one for the old folks! The funny part is that when the professor returned to the next class date, she said "I hope you all got the message that I posted" and not one person said a word. It wasn't long after that I began receiving emails from a couple of students asking questions about homework or exams. I never sought to find out who they were and we didn't really know each other in class by name. Call me over sensitive, but I thought it best to keep it as an email electronic classmate to classmate relationship.

If you look at any college website, you can get a wealth of information. Surprisingly or not the Department of Education's website is one of the worst to negotiate of all government websites; go figure. If you are thinking about teaching as a career change, find someone to talk to in person. The Department of Education's website is useless as tits on a bull. In this generation you can enroll, register, chose classes and find out about extra curricula activities at the push of a finger. The trouble is you have to be patient and don't get frustrated easily, because for security purposes primarily, you will have to go through several steps and even then it doesn't always work like it should. Make suggestions if you know the right people to contact. It took me about 4 hours to register for some classes on-line and that may sound like a long time but consider the alternative; I would have had to drive to campus or take the subway or bus, lug a lot of papers and forms, pay for parking or get a ticket, walk from site to site and probably lose my temper publically instead of privately. You do the math!

An area that could stand improvement is the method of putting registration holds on your account to satisfy obligations before registering for classes. Since we do have the benefit of electronic messaging it would be easy to notify students in advance of registering that they need to satisfy certain requirements which could be accomplished during the summer. I confess I do like receiving my grades over the internet. It sure beats the old way of a bunch of students huddled around a classroom door trying to match their grade with their student ID number. Basically your grades are confidential as well they should be.

Some professors make much better use of electronic media than others. It is a much better system to be able to interact with a professor or department administrator electronically than making an appointment to meet at an office. There are some things, just like in the business world that have to accomplished face-to-face. Financial issues come to mind immediately. There is no substitution for human contact when you're talking money.

Electronic record keeping is another invaluable tool. Promises are made and promises are broken, but an email acknowledgement is as good as any legal document written of paper, and a lot more reliable than a verbal promise. I remember where an issue can up about an assignment that the professor thought she had assigned, but as it turned, she had not. This is where old school integrity paid off. The professor came to me and asked what I had in my notes because she knew I wrote down everything and she took me at my word when I said I had no record of the assignment. Since I transfer notes to a word program every evening, I was able to verify my claim. This professor was no slacker and even though she gave me the benefit of the doubt and she acquiesced on my veracity, but secretly I think she still thought she had not made a mistake. That one assignment had the power to change grade outcomes by at least one letter grade. Professors for the most part are not out to screw the students. I believe she gave us a couple of other assignments to make up for the missing one. It didn't matter because I think all of the students would agree that her goal was to educate, not player hate.

If you are slightly computer savvy, you can track your performance weekly so that you can determine those areas of study where you need to work harder. You can prevent catastrophic failure before the final exam period. Grades are generally calculated on a point system, so you can develop an Excel worksheet to keep a running tally of your performance. Around mid-term exams you should be able to predict with some accuracy where you are going. That is not always the case, because professors factor in other measures of your performance which can either make you or break you. I grew up with the old adage; don't leave money lying on the table. If you can get extra points, at least in my case, get them. Treat this experience like a business and that's where you have an advantage of sorts, because through the years you should have learned how the game is played. If you want to feel you are making a contribution to the educational system, believe me the younger students are watching you.

Chapter 9
Overcoming Pitfalls and Perils

Up until now, I've painted a side of the picture that is full of optimism and makes it seem like everything just falls into place, just like you want it. Reality dictates that everything in life has upsides and downsides. The object is to weigh all of your options and determine the right fit for you. This is your life and no one has the right to dictate how you spend it. Spend is a good word to describe life, because it's a kind of currency that will eventually be exhausted. You get to chose where and how you want to spend it. You get to decide who and what you spend it on; you like fishing, you spend as much time doing that as possible, always keeping in the back of your head you are spending time, effort and money. The question is how much currency are you willing to spend on each pursuit. It's like if you ask someone out on date three or four times and they keep turning you down, then if you're smart you don't let them waste anymore of your currency.

Define what it is you want to do or to know. If you are like a lot of people I've met in life over a certain age, they feel that they know everything, been everywhere, seen everything and done everything. They don't want to learn anything, because they feel they don't need to ˼w anymore than they do now. We ought to all kick ourselves when ˼y that you don't know as much about computers as our children. ˼rself, is it because you don't need to know, don't want to know or too lazy to tax your brain to learn something new. Everyday parents say they can't help their children with their homework because they don't understand it. Well duh, it's time you learned it. Parents protest the teaching of evolution versus intelligent design not because they understand it, but because they believe it. Few people would want to analyze the facts, because it goes against what they think they know. These same people can't help their kid write a coherent paper for school, because they rely on what they have been taught or shown in the past and right or wrong; that is how it is done. That's beyond pathetic, that's dumb! In today's society, there really is no excuse for not being somewhat knowledgeable about almost any subject put before you. You have the ability to retrieve information at your fingertips. I used to sit in on meetings with people who were too lazy to research the background of the people that they were meeting with; most of the time these same people didn't even take notes. How do you expect to compete with the people who appreciate the value of reading and writing versus those that do not? If you have lost your zest for knowledge, shovel the dirt over yourself. As of this date, there are no such things as brain transplants. Even the rich can't buy one. You are stuck with the one you have been given. The beauty of it is that the brain has an unknown capacity for learning, but most people, rich or poor, black or white and every other color, get comfortable with using only a very small part of it.

Most of us have to work to make a living. Work requires spending the currency of time and energy; it does not matter if you're a ditch digger or a rocket scientist. Chances are if you are good at your job, you are mentally or physically exhausted by the end of your work cycle. This is where returning to school requires time management. If your routine is to come home, drink a beer, watch the news or chatting on-line, you have to figure out a way to halve those pursuits for school and study. Once again if you've already where you want to be there are no adjustments to be made. If you are one of those people who have thoughts about trying to make sense of your job or your life, you are probably are an ideal candidate for more formal education. If you're like me and love to read than why not translate that energy into getting more certification on your favorite subject. This is the type of currency you can always use again and unlike most of the things we spend our currency on education is renewable and recyclable.

Without detailing all of the programs out there, I can say categorically that there is probably some form of financial assistance to go back to school. A lot of jobs will contribute to going to school. With the exception of a few people, I have only met a few people who take advantage of these offers; including the GI Bill. The question is, do you want it or not? Over the years I have owned three, five and seven series BMW's. That's what I wanted and that's how I spent some of my currency, both time and money. If you can buy or lease a car, there is a way to finance returning to school. If you can't afford a car, chances are you might have an easier chance of financing school and if you have enough money to pay cash for a car then it just boils down to what is of value. Every college or university that I can think of has night and day classes. Schedules are adaptable. The professors I know are very accommodating. Thanks to the internet you can get a degree on-line. You have to lay out a roadmap just like you would do to plan for anything else that takes time and money. There will be sacrifices and there will be naysayers. It's a little like getting married, everybody has an opinion about it; what to wear, where to do it and the type of food you should serve at the reception; but if you want to be happy listen to them very cautiously.

One of the things I've learned quite vividly about myself is that I do my best thinking in the worst of times and I do my worst thinking in the best of times. When things are easy you rarely put a lot of thought into them. This recession has been a God-send, because I've discovered new ways to adapt and dreams and goals have resurfaced that I had long suppressed. I actually thank God now that it has happened and you can learn a lot about your own character in a storm.

If you are the kind of person who makes excuses for a lot of things not getting done than take a minute of time and look back on some of the things you gave up on in the past. The means test is whether or not you can blame some external force for preventing you from reaching your goal. External obstacles can be overcome if you are willing to go around them, over or through them. How bad do you want it?

An old guy I knew used to collect aluminum cans to sell for recycling. He used to throw his cans into an abandoned house in the city that had the first floor torn out so that everything went straight into the basement. His buddies used to make fun of him because he said his goal was to fill that basement up to the first floor with cans. His friends would say that it would take forever, but he kept right on going. Sometimes people would steal a bag or two out to sell for themselves, but they only had a short term goal, usually to get some cigarettes or bottle of wine. My old friend had a bigger picture in mind and he kept on going. A lot sooner than expected he had filled up the basement until cans were coming out of the front door. The recycle company provided a truck and some help and he loaded a couple of truck loads with smashed aluminum cans. I don't know how much he got altogether, but he was able to remodel his kitchen and bathroom in his house and had spending money left over. He did all this from picking up other people's trash and sticking to his goal. He wouldn't let anything or anybody get in his way, not even thieves could rob him of his dream. People talked about him, called him crazy and some people contributed by throwing cans in as well, mainly to mock him, but they didn't know he was laughing inside. He benefited from other peoples ignorance and evil. I learned a valuable lesson from that old man.

Chapter 10
Exhilaration

When the end of the semester came around and final exams were being held, I experienced the equalizer that made me forget all about my age and almost everything else. I had the same anxiety as my classmates, working hard to make the grade. Talk about re-awakened feelings; I had forgotten what it feels like to be so dependent on all of my hard work to come down to a finish line that is not elastic. Business goals are different because you can step back and rework a problem, bid on a new contract or change your business plan. Schools and learning are about winning or losing, either you know it or you don't. I cannot remember how many slips of paper I had scratched out possible scenarios about what my grades would be. I had to burn the mid-night oil like everybody else to study and not to be overly optimistic so I planned for the worst case. I knew I had done good enough to make a respectable showing, but I wanted some gold. Basically I had looked at each class from every angle; I was looking at it through a businessman's eyes. My best guess was that I might end up with a 3.0 average or with a little luck a 3.2. My daughter kept telling me that those are respectable grades especially from an old man (she didn't say it), that had been out of school for a number of years. After the finals were over and all of us waited for grades to be posted, I relaxed in the knowledge that I had worked hard and I had a good time doing it. The interaction with the professors, administrators and especially the students was the thrill of a lifetime. I truly felt like I had fit in and was not made out to be the freak I thought I would be in the beginning. After the last final exam, I took myself downtown to a restaurant with outdoor seating and I treated myself to some Maryland crab cakes and a couple of Blue Moon beers. I turned a thirty minute lunch into a two hour private happy hour. When I left, I put some money in a homeless lady's cup and thanked God that I had my Lazarus experience. I had come back from the dead, from the people who just keep doing the same things to just make it instead of trying to put some innocent happiness back into their lives and achieve something greater. It was one of those moments where I said God if I die right now, I will have achieved a level of happiness I had forgotten was possible. "Thank you!"

Back to reality for the next few days while I waited for my grades to be posted on the private university website sent directly to me. I went to an Economics Development meeting related to my business and during introductions I talked more about returning to school than about how my business was doing. I probably bored the hell out of the other participants, but I didn't notice and didn't care. I felt good!

When I went home, I checked my school email account and I couldn't believe my eyes. I had four "A's" and one "C". I called my wife and my daughter and I can't remember who else. Growing up in a macho lifestyle, I would hardly ever use a word like exhilaration, but that's the only word that comes to mind that describes this feeling. This was better than a cold beer on a hot day after a 2 to 1 baseball game. This was better than being told that you had gotten a two dollar raise on a ten dollar job. This was better than being told that the pregnancy test came back negative after you've had four kids already. This was exhilaration!

Both of my parents are somewhere smiling down on me with pride about my perseverance. There are costs to be paid for waiting so long to come to the self revelation that I have always loved to learn. The rule of my father is still to always get the facts. My mother passed away two days before completion of this chapter. Her words would be to ask me; what's next? If for nothing else I want my wife, son and daughter to know that it's never too late to learn and never to late to realize a dream. The Bible says in 2nd Timothy 2nd Chapter, 2nd and 3rd Verses: To be Strong in Grace… (2) "And the things you have heard from me among many witnesses, commit these to faithful men who will be able to teach others also. (3) You therefore must endure hardship as a good soldier of Jesus Christ." In Verse 15; "Be diligent to present yourself approved to God, a worker who need not be ashamed, rightly dividing the word of truth." No matter what faiths or religion or the lack thereof and no matter at what age, let us all find justification through knowledge and from knowledge grow wisdom and from wisdom find peace.

To the students of Howard University and students of all ages everywhere, you have something that can be never be replaced and cannot be achieved through forgery. This opportunity you have is a gift that must be returned in service. To those of us who do not think that they have the financial, physical or mental resources to become a student; teach them and those who don't know the joy learning; lead by example. Let not your laughter and joy go unacknowledged as not being based in the peace that comes from truth.

Manufactured By: RR Donnelley
Breinigsville, PA USA
January, 2011